Rooted

In Love

Table of Contents

Week One: The Father's Love

Day 1 Unfathomable Love

Day 2 Merciful Love

Day 3 Faithful Love

Day 4 Mighty Love

Day 5 Perfect Love

Day 6 Revealing Love

Day 7 Courageous Love

Week Two: Identity

Day 1 No Longer an Orphan

Day 2 New Creation

Day 3 Accepted

Day 4 Conqueror

Day 5 His Masterpiece

Day 6 Secure

Day 7 Blessed

Week Three: Purpose/Destiny

Day 1 Destined

Day 2 Trust

Day 3 Working Together

Day 4 Made To Accomplish

Day 5 Everything You Need

Day 6 My Might

Day 7 No Eye Has Seen

Week Four: Roots

Day 1 The Vine

Day 2 Love

Day 3 Faith

Day 4 Peace

Day 5 Wisdom

Day 6 Joy

Day 7 Hope

Introduction

For so many years I struggled to truly grasp the meaning and understanding of the love of God. I was so full of fear. I didn't love myself, and couldn't fathom why God would love me. Fear is intended to make you believe things that are not true.

The love of God is the most powerful force that will ever exist. It's powerful because God is love (1John 4:8). We were created in love and for love. When you truly encounter the love of God it will transform everything about you. For too long we've believed God is angry, and wants to punish us. That's a lie. God loves us so much, more than we can fathom. He couldn't stand the thought of you and I being separated from Him. He made a way so you and I could be in relationship with Him.

The love of God has a way of grounding and rooting us. It establishes our identity, purpose, and foundation. I pray as you go through this devotional; you'll encounter the love of God in a way you've never experienced, that will bring transformation

. ~Madeline James

"I also pray that love may be the ground into which you sink your roots and on which you have your foundation. This way, with all God's people you will be able to understand how wide, long, high, and deep His love is. You will know Christ's love, which goes far beyond any knowledge" Ephesians 3:17-19 (GW).

Week One: The Father's Love

Day 1

Unfathomable Love

For God so loved the world that He gave His only son, that whoever believes in Him should not perish but have eternal life. John 3:16

I so loved you, I gave My only son in exchange for you. I couldn't stand the thought of you being separated from Me for eternity. My love will do anything for you.

There is nothing that can separate you from My love. I will always move heaven and earth to bring you back to my heart. You are an expression of My heart. My love made a way for you to always be with Me.

Day 2

Merciful Love

But you, O Lord, are a merciful and gracious, slow to anger and abounding in steadfast love. Psalm 86:15

I am not angry with you. I love you. I don't sit on My throne waiting for you to mess up, so I can scold you. I am not a moody Father. My love for you never falters. It's steadfast and unchanging. There is no end to My love and grace for you. Nothing you'll ever do will cause My mercy and grace to run out. My love is enough to cover your sin. I forgive you.

Day 3

Faithful Love

Know therefore that the Lord your God is God; he is the faithful God, keeping his covenant of love to a thousand generations of those who love him and keep his commands. Deuteronomy 7:9

I keep my promises. I am not a

Father who lies to His children.

You can count on Me to always

follow through. Even when you

make mistakes, it does not cancel the promises I made to you. The display of My faithfulness to you, will be a testimony of the kind of Father I am. My faithfulness is not based on your ups and downs. It's because I love you, and that will never change.

Day 4

Mighty Love

The Lord your God in your midst, The Mighty One will save; He will rejoice over you with gladness, He will quiet you with His love, He will rejoice over you with singing. Zephaniah 3:17

I am always with you. You may not always feel Me or sense My presence, but I'm always there.

You are not alone in the battles you face. The power of My love is enough for every battle. Allow My love to quiet your heart. Trust Me. My songs will bring deliverance. I love to sing and dance over you. It's My favorite thing. Nothing can stop the power of My love. I love you child.

Day 5

Perfect Love

God is love. Whoever lives in love lives in God, and God in them. There is no fear in love. But perfect love drives out fear.

1 John 4:16, 18

Live inside of My love. It's the safest place to be. My love surrounds every part of you. You are safe from the demons and thoughts that torment you. Fear cannot exist where My love is. Allow My love to expel every ounce of fear that exist in you. You were made in love, and for love. Fear does not come from Me. I am a loving Father. Allow My love to take all your fears away.

Day 6

Revealing Love

Call to me and I will answer you and show you great and mighty things, which you do not know. Jeremiah 33:3

I'm waiting for you. I want to take you places you've never been before. I long to show you the mysteries and secrets of My heart.

Do you trust Me to take where you've never been? It's My delight to share My secrets with those who are hungry for more. Are you hungry? Do you desire to know more of Me? I'm ready when you are. Just call My name.

Day 7

Courageous Love

Don't be afraid, for I am with you. Don't be discouraged, for I am your God. I will strengthen you and help you. Isaiah 41:10

Don't be fearful child, I am here with you. You will never face anything alone. I will always be with you. Allow courage to rise up deep within you. You will not be overcome by what you're facing, or what's come after you. I did not give you the spirit of fear, but of love and power, and a sound mind (2 Timothy 1:7). I made you to be courageous. Go be courageous! I am with you.

Week 2: Identity

Day 1

No Longer An Orphan

So you have not received a spirit that makes you fearful slaves. Instead, you received God's Spirit when he adopted you as his own children. Now we call him, "Abba, Father." For His Spirit joins with our spirit to affirm that we are God's children. Romans 8:15-16

You are no longer an orphan. You are My child, and nothing can change that. Don't allow fear to rule in your heart. Let My love rule in you. I have not pushed you away, but have drawn you close. You have found a place in My family. Nothing can ever take that place away from you. You are mine.

Day 2

New Creation

This means that anyone who belongs to Christ has become a new person. The old life is gone; a new life has begun. 2Corinthians 5:17

There's no need to look over your shoulder anymore. You have been made new in Me. I no longer see your past, or who you were before you came to Me. All you've ever done has been covered under My blood. You are free. Free to be who I created you to be. Everything has been made new.

Day 3

Accepted

To praise of the glory of His grace, by which He made us accepted in the Beloved. Ephesians 1:6

My child look no further for your acceptance. You are accepted in Me. The sting of rejection no longer has to haunt you. I do not love like those around you. Accept

My love as I've accepted you. My love is all encompassing. You no longer have to wander around looking for the love and acceptance you crave. There is no striving in My love. You are accepted. I love everything about you.

Day 4

More Than a Conqueror

What then shall we say in response to these things? If God is for us, who can be against us? No in all things we are more than conquerors through him who loved us. Romans 8:31, 37

You are not called to live a life of defeat, but a life of victory. The enemy wants you to believe the lie you can't overcome the situations and people that come against you. But that's what I created you to be, a conqueror. You were made to overcome. Don't fear when the enemy or situations rise up against you. I have placed inside you the ability to conquer. You are more than able.

Day 5

His Masterpiece

For we are God's masterpiece. He has created us anew in Christ Jesus, so we can do the good things he for us long ago. Ephesians 2:10

You are not ordinary. You are uniquely made. I took My time on you. Each and every detail is handcrafted. Nothing about you is a mistake or unimportant. You are

My masterpiece. I was intentional about every part of you I put together. What you thought you lost or didn't have has been made new. Everything you need to accomplish what I've called you to do has, already been placed inside of you.

Day 6

Secure

He who dwells in the secret place of the Most High shall remain stable and fixed under the shadow of the Almighty. Psalm 91:1

There will come many situations and circumstances that will invade in your life. To survive and come out on the other side of your circumstances, it's imperative you dwell in the secret place with Me. I will keep you stable and secure, so you won't be swept away by what comes your way. I am the safest place. You're security is found only in Me. Anything other than Me will leave you exposed. Come and dwell under the safety of My shadow My child.

Day 7

Blessed

Surely your goodness and unfailing love will pursue me all the days of my life. Psalm 23:6

My child I wish you understood just how blessed and favored you are. If you knew, you would walk different. It's My desire to help you discover My goodness and love. It's not something you earn. I declared it over your life from the day I formed you. You can't out run My goodness, love, and mercy, or exhaust it. If you let Me, I will overtake you with all I am. I am a good Father. You will forever be blessed with My love, goodness, and all I am. Nothing can change who I am, or who you are.

Week Three:

Purpose/Destiny

Day 1

Destined

For I know the plans I have for you, says the Lord. They are plans for good and not disaster, to give you a future and a hope. Jeremiah 29:11

It may seem like you're not going in the right direction, or you missed it. You've not missed it. From the foundations of the earth, I have destined you for greatness. My plans are full of goodness and hope, not the disaster you fear. Come and sit with Me. I want to tell you about the things I've planned for your life. Don't be afraid to dream. I've put those desires and longings in your heart. Your future is bright.

Day 2

Trust

Trust in the Lord with all your heart; do not depend on your own understanding. Seek his will in all you do, and he will show you which path to take. Proverbs 3:5-6

Destiny requires trust. It's not a destination, but a journey with Me. Destiny will unfold with each step we take together. The steps I ask you to take won't always make sense. Trust Me. It's going to be a fun, unpredictable, and sometimes a bumpy journey. You can trust me, because I see the big picture. I know where we have to go, and what paths will lead to the destiny and purpose I've created you for. Trust me. Daddy knows best.

Day 3

Working It Together

And we know that God causes everything to work together for the good of those who love God and are called according to His purpose for them. Romans 8:28

Don't fear My child. There is a lot going on behind the scenes that will eventually come to the forefront. If you could see now what will unfold, you would rejoice. Be patient. Trust Me. I'm not intentionally causing you to suffer. I'm purposefully putting all things together. No experience you've had will ever be wasted. It's coming together now. I've had to build you one experience at a time, to ensure you can walk in the fullness of My purpose for you.

Day 4

Made To Accomplish

So will My word be which goes out of My mouth; it will not return to Me void without it accomplishing what I desire, and without succeeding in the matter for which I sent it. Isaiah 55:11

The words I have spoken over your life will come to pass. It may not always be in your timing, but will be in My timing. I am always faithful to perform what I send forth. My words will not hit the ground. Keep speaking the words I have spoken over you My child. Remind yourself of My promises. I have placed My promises inside you and over you. I have destined you to accomplish all I have set out for you.

Day 5

Everything You Need

For we are God's masterpiece. He has created us anew in Christ Jesus, so we can do the good things he planned for us long ago. Ephesians 2:10

I know you feel inadequate at times, and feel like you don't have what it takes. Be confident My child, I have masterfully woven and imparted everything you'll ever need to fulfill your destiny. When I planned out your days, I put every strategy, plan, book, thought, wisdom, etc., inside of you. As you diligently seek Me, I will reveal each of those of that right time. Everything you need is found in Me.

Day 6

My Might

You won't succeed by might or by power, but by My Spirit says the Lord of hosts. Zechariah 4:6

You won't be able to walk out your destiny in your own strength. You're going to think you can, but you won't make it. I Am the wind and the force that will cause the chain reactions and the open doors. Anything you do in your own strength, you'll have to keep in your strength. I Am the force that will propel you forward and make things happen. Sit back and watch Me work.

Day 7

No Eye Has Seen

No eye has seen, no ear has heard, and no mind has imagined what God has prepared for those who love Him.
1Corinthians 2:9

You think you have an idea of where I'm taking you. But My child you have no idea the things I have planned for you. Don't be afraid to dream with Me, because I have placed those dreams and desires within you first. Anything you can dream of is only a glimpse of what I've planned and desire for you. Trust Me as I lead you. Get ready to see my extravagant love and goodness displayed in your life.

Week Four: Roots

Day 1

The Vine

Yes, I am the vine; you are the branches. Those who remain in me, and I in them, will produce much fruit. For apart from me you can do nothing.
John 15:5

I am your source. It's important where you decide to plant yourself. You can't put your roots down just anywhere. Be intentional. Plant yourself in Me, and you will never have to worry about being barren or fruitless. I am the source of life and stability you need. Allow Me to be a part of your life. You can't do this alone. Together there are endless possibilities.

Day 2

Love

Then Christ will live in you through faith. I also pray that love may be the ground into which you sink your roots and on which you have your foundation. This way, with all of God's people you'll be able to understand how wide, long, high, and deep His love is. Ephesians 3:17-18

In order to be grounded in who you are, you must be grounded in My love. Love is the foundation of everything you do. My love will never change for you. Your value and My love for you will never change. It was set from the beginning and confirmed on the cross. Sink your roots down deep in my love for you. The further you go the more you'll realize how great My love is for you.

Day 3

Faith

Let your roots grow down into him, and let your lives be built on him. Then your faith will grow strong in the truth you were taught, and you will overflow with thankfulness. Colossians 2:7

Faith will take you many places. It makes a way when there seems to be no way. Faith calls things into existence that were not. To truly walk in the Spirit, you must walk by faith, and not by what you see or don't see. The only way faith can truly operate in a powerful way in your life, is through trust. Your trust must be rooted in Me. You'll only go as high as the depth of your trust is in Me.

Day 4

Peace

You will keep in perfect peace all who trust in you, all whose thoughts are fixed on you. Isaiah 26:3

When you root yourself in Me, I will give you a peace that will exceed your understanding. Many times your emotions and thoughts are like a stormy sea. Rooting yourself in Me, gives you the ability to let go of the things and situations that steal your peace. Being grounded in Me allows you to remain calm when everything around you is raging. My peace can go down to the deepest parts of who you are because you are rooted in Me.

Day 5

Wisdom

Give me an understanding heart so that I can govern your people well and know the difference between right and wrong.   1 Kings 3:9

Desire wisdom, for it is the principle thing. Wisdom will be your safeguard. In this hour there are many deceptions, lies, and false motives roaming about. Wisdom will enable you to know the difference and discern what is true. My counsel will guide your steps along the right path. Wisdom will give you the strategy to win the battle. Don't be wise in your own eyes. Root yourself in Me, and trust my counsel. I see the end from the beginning.

Day 6

Joy

*The joy of the Lord is your strength.
Nehemiah 8:10*

Let your joy run down deep in me. When you are rooted in Me, I will give you unspeakable joy. It will cause you to laugh in the face of insurmountable circumstances. My joy allows you to laugh, because it knows who God is. Worry, fear, and anxiety will sap your strength. Tap into My joy, and you'll find the strength you need to make it through your trials. You can laugh because the battle has already been won on the cross.

Day 7

Hope

To them God has chosen to make know among the gentiles the glorious riches of this mystery, which is Christ in you, the hope of glory. Colossians 1:27

I AM the Hope of Glory that lives in you. You can always have hope because of what I did on the cross. Allow hope to root you in your circumstances. As the days go on it will grow dark, but take heart. Hope lives inside you and will help you see from My perspective. Like My love, My hope never gives up because it's rooted in love. Be a beacon of hope to those around you. Many will throw their hope away as things grow darker. Let your hope shine bright as you anchor yourself in Me.

References

The Bible http://www.thebible.com

Made in United States
Orlando, FL
28 November 2023